GOD OF NOTHINGNESS

ALSO BY MARK WUNDERLICH

The Anchorage

Voluntary Servitude

The Earth Avails

God of Nothingness

POEMS

Mark Wunderlich

GRAYWOLF PRESS

This publication is made possible, in part, by the voters of Minnesota through a Minnesota State Arts Board Operating Support grant, thanks to a legislative appropriation from the arts and cultural heritage fund. Significant support has also been provided by Target Foundation, the McKnight Foundation, the Lannan Foundation, the Amazon Literary Partnership, and other generous contributions from foundations, corporations, and individuals. To these organizations and individuals we offer our heartfelt thanks.

Published by Graywolf Press
250 Third Avenue North, Suite 600
Minneapolis, Minnesota 55401

www.graywolfpress.org

Published in the United States of America

ISBN 978-1-64445-042-0

2 4 6 8 9 7 5 3 1
First Graywolf Printing, 2021

Library of Congress Control Number: 2020937393

Cover design: Carlos Esparza

Cover art: Franz Sedlacek, *Storm* (detail), 1932. Photo © Belvedere, Vienna.

for Douglas Culhane

Contents

Now he understood her, who had lived beside him
so many years and been loved but never understood.
You were never truly together with one you loved
until the person in question was dead and actually
inside you.

—*Thomas Bernhard*

Strange, not to go on wishing one's wishes. Strange
to see what was once so connected
drifting in space.

—*Rainer Maria Rilke*

GOD OF NOTHINGNESS

I.

WUNDERLICH

The name means "odd."
The name means "queer."
It can denote an "odd fish."
It suggests a "queer chap."
Sometimes it means "capricious." It can also mean "peevish."
It's a synonym for "singular." It is thought to be poetic.
The Pied Piper of Hamelin was called *ein wunderlicher Kauz*,
with his colorful clothing come to pipe the rats away.
He drowned them in the Weser, or so the stories go.
When the mayor withheld payment
he took the children and drowned them with the rats,
or perhaps they went into the mountains,
or they moved to Transylvania.
"It is one-hundred years since our children left,"
says the crumbling book found in the church—
that is what it means to be a Wunderlich.
The name means "strange things happened to him."
It means "he can be disputatious."
It means he sometimes wears peculiar garments to a party,
that as he aged, he seemed younger, less reliable,
more in touch with what he would call his "soul."
(You might not call it that yourself.)
It can mean "quarrelsome."
It can mean "he prefers cats."
It can mean he has a gnome tattooed
near the hair underneath his arm.
It means "he loves Christmas like a simpleton."
It means "makes sushi out of SPAM."
The name means "curious," as in "he bought a haunted house,"
and since weaning, he's not touched a woman's breast.
It means "he loves the color orange." It means "he studied Dutch."
It means pancakes for supper once again this week,
and that he prefers to knit his own socks.
The name means "electric organ maestro."

The name means "famous botanical illustrator."
It means the drunken tenor ass-over-teakettle down a set of Viennese stairs.
It is true there are few of us, that we spread ourselves thin around the globe;
find us making wine in Hungary, herding cattle in Namibia,
captaining a ship somewhere off the Chilean coast.
My Wunderlichs steamed up the long brown Mississippi
in a boat that put them and their peculiarities off in Wisconsin
where the name means a shady farm
growing a crop of moss on a roof,
an old man with a pistol in his pants,
a child who didn't survive and occupies
a pagan's ashy grave atop a limestone bluff
where the wind speaks his strange name or worse—
voices recognition, an attribution, or a curse.

A DRIFTLESS SON

It came to me to sell the family farm,
shift its failures to a man who planned

to occupy the place for recreation,
to hunt the deer that spook and shadow in the pines,

my job to consign to another my granddad's stunted grove
of walnuts planted—against the forester's advice—

with his hired man Tiny, who died
by stepping in front of a train, though first he roped

his dog Bear to a nearby tree, tacking on a note
that read "Take Care Off Me." Does anyone

remember this fat fact—a loaf of toast and a dozen eggs
was Tiny's daily breakfast meal? Give it

to me. I'll remember that bit too. I fished
that muddy pond just once, its manurey slurry

slipped downstream
from the Tulius brothers' hogs,

shot the one buck trophied on my wall
whose crippled hoof had slowed him

dangerously down. In town again
I pulled the locks off all the doors of the barn—

empty now, October now,
the deer not yet come to any harm.

HA HA LITTLE HUNCHBACK

Ha ha little hunchback—look at him pretend to trip,
teeth in his pocket, ring the doorbell three times

and make the children clap! He taught me
to run the bandsaw and run the chainsaw,

cut a key from a blank key, how to break into a car
through the window without breaking the window.

He fixed slot machines and gumball machines,
made mechanical decoys with pulleys and weights.

Verstehst du, Bub? he'd ask, and I'd nod
but I usually didn't understand the little hunchback.

At nine I couldn't drive so he taught me to drive.
We'd cruise the corn stubble with the noses

of our midget guns poked out the windows of the Jeep.
His: The Black Prince, mine: Little Red Fox,

blocks on the pedals so both of us could reach.
We'd shoot squirrels and we'd shoot ruffed grouse

and when I shot a pheasant cock, he had the feathers
made into a fancy band for a hat.

"Good enough for who it's for," he'd say,
tapping in a crooked carpentry nail.

He made his money in moonshine sugar,
made his money making bad luck loans,

hired a giant everyone called Tiny
then he became Tiny's home.

His teeth pinched so he didn't wear them,
his idea of a lady's gift was a meat slicer he knew

she'd have to wash, but who wouldn't want to ponder
a moon of pink bologna slipped fresh into an outstretched palm?

As a child he'd hitch up his angry pony
and beat it all the way to the train

to fetch the bales of tobacco and haul them to the shop.
If he dawdled and was late, Grandpa Adolf

would unbuckle his wooden leg
and leave it napping on a chair,

then beat his little hunchback with a cane—
Little Hunchback, Little Hunchback,

never you be late again!

HAUNTED HOUSE

I moved into the haunted house
and gutted it to the bones. I wasn't alone then,

and worked there in a team.
We evicted squirrels from their vast nutshell nest,

filled dumpsters with fifty years of trash.
I found three lit and ornamented trees in a pile of brush,

uncovered secret drawings in a drawer.
We tore up a floor to uncover a floor,

sanded tulip poplar to a sheen. I let
the others unhouse the rat snake

muscled around the boiler pipes downstairs.
They took it in a pail to Corlaer's Creek

where it braided angrily away. I too
slithered in the muddy crawlspace,

headlamp sputtering with sweat.
When the house began to wake,

the strangers began to arrive, driving their cars
up our long drive to have a proper snoop.

Uninvited, they told of Dutch Mary
rocking in her scarf, dead slaves

buried in a hollow up the hill, the wellhead
by the Indian trail where carriages stopped

to let their long-dead horses have a drink.
If you think this scared me, you'd be wrong.

I know a story meant to frighten when I hear one.
Now I live here alone with the spirits I cannot see.

I spend my days inside these rubble stone walls
cooking small meals and stoking logs into a smoking stove

while around me history stills to pictures in a frame—
the same clouded view for Old Dutch Mary

waiting at the window once again.

GONE IS GONE

for Lucie Brock-Broido

I was there at the edge of Never,
of Once Been, bearing the night's hide

stretched across the night sky,
awake with myself disappointing myself,

armed, legged & torsoed in the bed,
my head occupied by enemy forces,

mind not lost entire, but wandering
off the marked path ill-advisedly. This March

Lucie upped & died, & the funny show
of her smoky-throated world began to fade.

I didn't know how much of me was made
by her, but now I know that this spooky art

in which we staple a thing
to our best sketch of a thing was done

under her direction, & here I am
at 4 a.m., scratching a green pen over a notebook

bound in red leather in October.
It's too warm for a fire. She'd hate that.

And the cats appear here only as apparitions
I glimpse sleeping in a chair, then

Wohin bist du entschwunden? I wise up,
know their likenesses are only inked

on my shoulder's skin, their chipped ash poured
in twin cinerary jars downstairs. *Gone*

     is gone, said the goose to the shrunken boy
in the mean-spirited Swedish children's book

     I love. I shouldn't be writing this
at this age or any other. She mothered

     a part of me that needed that, lit
a spirit-lantern to spin shapes inside

     my obituary head, even though—
I'm nearly certain now—she's dead.

WOODEN BOX

for John DiCarlo

John's ashes flew from Stockholm in a box
Anders stowed in the overhead compartment,

brought it across the ocean to Provincetown,
and when he put it down on the little side table

it's as if a cloud formed and we all went solemn
as an absence filled the house. He was there

by not being there, more thought than form,
like the hardbacked books coffined on the shelves.

The box stood sentinel throughout the day
while guests ate oysters and sipped champagne.

Someone played the piano and others sang
and after the sun had set and we mourners had our say

we carried the box to the Breakwater where—
illegally we knew—we would consign him to the bay.

Someone scooped some ash into a pill bottle
to keep some portion on their shelf.

I did not. Did not want to keep a bit
of that body here, so far beyond permission,

wanted him gone from this place as he did,
the noose that took him a looping final script.

In the dark, Anders clambered down the slippery rocks
clutching the box to his chest.

No one spoke as John was poured out into the bay,
the ashes washed with mud and sand—

unwritten in this way.

ONCE FORGOTTEN

The old woman kept the tulip bulbs in the basement to keep them from the musk-rats, overwintered the geraniums in a barrel. She fed the water snake who lived in the boathouse, flicking him little stars of meat, which he rose up to catch, his body black as the night's shadow. When we played down in the storm sewers and didn't come home, she walked through town and shouted into the grates, "Tweety, are you down there?" She didn't care. When she cleaned a carp, she kept the lucky stone from inside its head as a bingo chip, chopped the carp into chum. I bought her Chesterfields whenever she asked, and she smoked them in a blue fog in the kitchen, frying pan in the oven to keep the flavored grease. When she taught us to shoot, she took us to the dump so we could practice on unlucky rats, she taught us to clean sunfish and crappies and pike. When we needed a puppet she sewed us a puppet, when we were sick, she fed us peppermint schnapps. The old woman kept a broken porcelain doll and a thick severed braid in the cedar chest at the foot of her twin bed—pure *sentimentia*. "Shit or get off the pot," she said as we played penny ante with ourselves. Her house by the river shook from the trains, the barge lights stroked the dark bedroom in the night. She made turkeys with pinecones and pipe cleaners, glued sequins onto Styrofoam balls. Once she made kolaches but never again; the pork roast was always smothered in kraut. And when she forgot she forgot all of it—forgetting to eat, forgetting to dress, forgetting even where she was, waking up wet and cold on the floor. Me? She forgot me too. Wind blew through the pines out on the sand prairie, and that was what she became. She forgot me and I was forgettable. Once forgotten I could walk away and be free.

SHANTY

No one remembers what became of the people
in the house now swaybacked in the marsh—

not the mice whispering and tunneled in the couch,
not the snapping turtle armored on a log

retracting his hard beak into wrinkled folds like foreskin.
Not my mother who visited the shanty once as a nurse,

noting the packed dirt floor, the walls pasted up in newsprint.
They burnt waste oil in a barrel stove they got free from a garage,

dipped their water from a spring now greened with cress.
Ardys Keilholtz knew something of the wife

but couldn't think—*what was she called to home?*
When I was small, I heard roosters crowing from their yard

and think I rode a school bus with the girl,
but now I couldn't say for sure.

Bill Wendt taught me to trap muskrats in that swamp,
staking a Conibear in the muddy muskrat runs with brush.

I pulled their plush-furred bodies from the ice,
sold them for cash money to the fur man in the spring.

How long will I keep telling stories just like this—
dirt floors and traplines and a shack abandoned in a swamp?

The vividness of that world is fading like my father's addled mind.
Poverty is not poetry, this I know. But these pictures

are what's left of childhood and now all my male relatives are gone
though lost and half-remembering—my father—living on.

CHATEAU ON AN ISLAND IN A LAKE

In late summer I drove half the day to the Cape,
came to the end of that sandy arm,
slept the night upstairs at the White Horse Inn

and dreamed it was my job to escort Lucie through a wood,
walking a path snaked with roots, to a shallow lake
ringed with a beach of stones. In the lake was an island

and on that island rose a turreted chateau
gloomy in its isolation—our destination.
A ringlet of smoke curled up from a chimney,

and lights lit the upper chambers of the house.
I searched for a bridge or a ferry to take us over
but all that remained were timbers bobbing

where a bridge once spanned. I looked down
at Lucie's shoes, cobbled according to her specific whims,
beautiful and witchy in their willfulness

and couldn't bear to see them ruined, and so
I told her to climb up on my back
so I could carry her across. "You hardly weigh a thing,"

I said, wading into the water, which was cold
as I had expected. As my legs broke the glassy stillness
with my passenger on my back, I awoke.

Outside, the tide was coming in, green curtains
breathed out at the window of my room,
lake gone, chateau disappearing into memory,

and Lucie nowhere to be found.

THE PRODIGAL

> A certain man had two sons . . .
>> *Luke 15:11*

I am the one who stayed, did as he was told, remained
behind with his straight A's, Goody-Two-Shoes, Mr. Butter-Wouldn't-Melt.

I felt all the resentment stockpiled by anyone that clean
and good, with my organized calendar, color-coded tabs, balanced

checkbook, money in the bank. Unthanked, I took the old women
to church, lurched through the Fellowship Hall

to clean up after Volunteer Lunch.
It was I who put down the incontinent dog,

drove the old man to Rochester through sleet,
then went to work, managed the accounts,

sold off the machinery and got a good price.
It must be nice to be so very absent, not return the call,

spending fall and winter doing as he pleased,
dancing high and costumed in the desert dust,

Burning Man's skeleton ablaze. Meanwhile on planet Earth
I got the leaves cleaned up and prepared to shovel snow.

Here I go, back to Lake Winona Manor, to mush through another hour
of *Gunsmoke* and soft brown food, sipping a plastic cup of milk

while willing my bruise-colored mood away.
How easy it was to stay, to suffer nobly and alone,

how simple to be useful to the infirm,
keep the whispered vigil, pat the dying man's hand,

a relief to wake worried about the crop, spend the morning
oiling tools, sweeping up the shop

while he spends the bail money I sent parachuting from a plane.
For years we didn't hear from him, though he cashed

the birthday check, while we imagined him as some wreck
sleeping on a bus. We. All of us.

And so he returned, welcomed warily by our dwindling clan,
to shake his dying dad's hand. Here I stand

in the background, frying the fatted calf in grease,
while he weeps for what was lost—for himself—

and with evident enviable release.

VISITATION

My mother is alive and funny
        in the house above the marsh.

I think she does not miss my father much
        as he is still alive, though elsewhere.

Now that the men and dogs are gone,
        the team of mules separated and sold off

to Iowa and Missouri, now
        that we put down the last Labrador—

a curly-coated giant stinking in the kitchen
        who loved a tennis ball arcing through the air

more than his keeper, more than ducks or food,
        more than rolling in some putrefaction—

now that the yard is quiet,
        the guns slumbering and locked in their closets,

the wild creatures have returned to the yard—
        the fork-horned buck gingers out of the woods

to eat the windfall apples, the woodchuck
        undermines the retaining wall, bats, squirrels, a coyote

printing his mute tracks in a loop around the house
        which is now locked in a feminine quiet

and where my mother reads, works her puzzles,
        clicks her needles as she knits another sweater

for a baby I'll never meet.
        I think she likes being unobserved—

husband gone, boys grown up strange
  and long since moved away. She does as she sees fit.

Now it is just the creatures who watch her
  come and go, like the bobcat she startled

when she stepped out on the porch
  who looked up, saw her, then disappeared into the trees.

He left no tracks, no whiff of musk or scat,
  and so my mother wonders to no one who will hear

if the cat was ever really there at all.

FIRST, CHILL

This year I did not love the first snow,
took no joy from the clean whiteness

masking the contours of my yard,
the last leaves stripped from the weeping beech

to reveal its looping undercarriage,
the ground hardened underfoot

as the world froze in late November.
I have secretly admired the first hard frost

killing the garden, putting an end
to its many failures, the beetles and rusts

finally put to death, and which are hard
not to see as moral judgments

on my insufficient diligence.
This year I put on the woolens,

banked the stove with oak and elm,
watched the snow feather down

on the spruce, the grass still green under white,
and I felt an uncommon dread

for the inward turn that usually marks these days
that end in early nights at home

with their firelit contemplations,
the darkened privacy of the lamp

encircling the pages of an open book.
I wanted more—not of summer,

with its swampy air and the nighttime
amphibian whir, but of autumn

with its metallic skies swept with clouds,
of the promise of something about to end,

but not yet taken away.
Above the Catskills, the peaks are veiled

in a cloud of snow. This is where
I think my dead have gone—

my father and Lucie and John—the dead
being impervious to cold,

having left their bodies with us to cherish,
but also to bury and to burn.

I imagine them as they wander the high peaks,
rippling like figures underwater,

like figures one dreams and forgets,
a shape drawn and erased

so only the pencil's impress remains.
Now that they are frozen

I know they are truly dead.
Let me let them go

I pray to the God of Nothingness
who rules those icy, bluestone peaks,

who hides the world of the living
underneath his coat of snow.

He has taken them from me
and now I will them, coldly, to go.

CUTHBERT

I had a lamb and named him Cuthbert.
Cuthbert was what I named my little lamb.

I fed him oats and I fed him corn.
I fed him on the clover flush with spring.

I pet and patted Cuthbert every day,
fed him on the brightest summer hay.

Cuthbert, little Cuthbert, how he grew.
I knew then what Cuthbert didn't know.

I trained Cuthbert daily for the fair,
led him with a gleaming halter in a ring.

Spring drew on, and dully led to summer.
My little lamb was now a market wether.

We took him in a trailer to the show.
He bedded down in bright sawdust in his stall.

I blackened Cuthbert's pretty cloven hooves.
I carded Cuthbert's haunches with a comb.

I oiled his black muzzle until it shone
and the day came to take him to the ring.

The livestock judge opened Cuthbert's mouth,
examined Cuthbert's single row of teeth.

He patted hands on Cuthbert's meaty loin,
moved us into a single showman's line.

The judge returned, walked off, came back again,
pulled us from the lineup and then said

this market wether was the finest in his class.
That night I put Cuthbert on the block.

The auctioneer sang the money from the crowd.
Cuthbert stood tensely and I was proud.

A banker bid the highest for the lamb.
I led him through the sawdust to his pen,

fed him a laudatory meal in his pan.

By morning the stalls stood empty in a row
and we children were invited to the show

of the carcasses of market lambs and hogs,
of Hereford steers trained docile as a dog.

The bodies stripped of hides hung on their hooks.
We filed past them casting furtive looks,

the carcasses' bright surfaces white with fat,
the room chilled cold enough so that

the meat we grew stayed incorruptible and fresh.
We exited the abattoir's cold light

and in the concrete hallway was the sight
of heads struck dumb and staring by the door

under plastic sheeting on the floor
to be taken to the mink farm we were told

for every precious portion had been sold.
His head looked out at nothing he could see.

Cuthbert, little Cuthbert, you have nothing left for me.

II.

MY NIGHT WITH JEFFREY DAHMER

—like any night spent out in a bar—this one
doused in the pink and blue of neon, 1989, Formica

and brushed metal and the spin of sound in the club
while downstairs in a darker bar, where the older men

enjoyed each other's company and where I had gone
to cool off, a man stood next to me

and knocked my beer to the floor—*so sorry*—he was
very sorry—hand on my arm as I bent to pick up

the bottle, one hand on my arm, the other signaling
to the bartender, holding up a finger then pointing

to the empty I proffered, put on the wooden counter,
bottle which the keep swept away, replaced,

a cold, green glass already sweating a bit, beading
in the heat of the basement.

He was a stranger, older than I was by a decade or more,
blond and mustached, big glasses—some farmer's son—

a bit out of date, stuck as he was in the country,
a man driven in to the capital, to spend a night

among others of his kind, away from his mother's kitchen,
the chilled hum of the bulk tank, and the cows

whose needs were at the center of a life spent in their service—
but no, he was from Milwaukee, he said, though to me

his words were unimportant—*so sorry, let me, I'll get you
a new one, let me buy you one*—

and so he took out his wallet and handed over his dollars
and I suppose I looked to see

if he had left a tip since I always look for this,
having done already the work of service

in which you depend on the manners and guilt
and sense of custom of those you attend, their

generosity, their goodness, their notion
of what is normal and right, what to offer to others

in exchange for their help, their attentiveness, *here
let me buy you a beer, so sorry for my clumsiness,*

*let me put this hand on your arm, do you live here,
are you at the University, do you like the music,*

did I tell you my name?—his questions the questions
of any curious man talking to a farmer's son

in a bar in Madison, Wisconsin, asking my name which I withheld,
my name which I keep lodged between my teeth,

under my tongue, in the pocket of my clavicle,
in the scar on my eyebrow, in my belly,

in the sack of my scrotum, in my head, my hand, my arm
which he touched lightly, my mouth, my teeth, my tongue

which began to move, unlock, give up its wariness, give in
to say, *my name is Mark. What's yours?*

GOD OF NOTHINGNESS

My father fell from the boat.
His balance had been poor for some time.

He had gone out in the boat with his dog
hunting ducks in a marsh near Trempealeau, Wisconsin.

No one else was near
save the wiry farmer scraping the gutters in the cow barn

who was deaf in one ear from years of machines—
and he was half a mile away.

My father fell from the boat
and the water pulled up around him, filled

his waders and this drew him down.
He descended into water the color of weak coffee.

The dog went into the water too,
thinking perhaps this was a game.

I must correct myself—dogs do not think as we do—
dogs react, and the dog reacted by swimming

around my father's head. This is not a reassuring story
about how the dog signaled for help by barking,

or by licking my father's face, encouraged him
to hold on. The dog eventually tired and went ashore

to sniff through the grass, enjoy his new freedom
from the attentions of his master,

indifferent to my father's plight.
The water was cold, I know that,

and my father has always chilled easily.
That he was cold is a certainty, though

I have never asked him about this event.
I do not know how he got out of the water.

I believe the farmer went looking for him
after my mother called in distress, and then drove

to the farm after my father did not return home.
My mother told me of this event in a hushed voice,

cupping her hand over the phone and interjecting
cheerful non sequiturs so as not to be overheard.

To admit my father's infirmity
would bring down the wrath of the God of Nothingness

who listens for a tremulous voice and comes rushing in
to sweep away the weak with icy, unloving breath.

But that god had been called years before
during which time he planted a kernel in my father's brain

which grew, freezing his tongue,
robbing him of his equilibrium.

The god was there when he fell from the boat,
whispering from the warren of my father's brain,

and it was there when my mother, noting the time,
knew that something was amiss. This god is a cold god,

a hungry god, selfish and with poor sight.
This god has the head of a dog.

THE SON I'LL NEVER HAVE

The son I'll never have is crossing the lawn. He is lying on an imaginary bed,

the coverlet pulled up over his knees—knees I don't dare describe.

I recoil from imagining him as meat and bone, as a mind

and hands stroking the fur of his pet rabbit.

I never gave him the accordion I used to play, my mother and I

in duets, "The Minnesota Polka," "What a Friend We Have in Jesus,"

never watched him push noodles into his mouth with fingers

while I wished he would use the spoon shiny with disuse.

I am free from longing to be free, I do as I please,

my money is my own, all the mistakes I make are only my mistakes.

What is it to look at something you made and see the future?

What is it to have someone made by your body, but whose mind

remains just out of reach? I'll never know. Come here, little rabbit.

Eat these greens. I will pet your cloudy fur with the mind's hand.

DEATH OF A CAT

Little beast on the metal table, she took
the needle into her forepaw

and didn't flinch. The medicinal death
fit itself inside her, ran the blue and red map,

burned up into her lungs and brain
and heart, which slowed,

and she slept until there was no breath left
and her body emptied itself of air.

A bit of blood showed at the nose,
and as her warmth left, her lungs and throat

rattled a little which was the sound
of the earth taking back the quickness

it had lent her. Eleven years had passed
inside her body, all of them as my companion,

having found her as a kitten shut up
in a cage. These are the years during which

I have lost a great deal, while the cat watched
in her dumb way, unburdened by the need

to assign language to everything she sees.
A man I loved left, and the household

we built together became a private realm
populated by my singularity, the paper city

of my books, and by this cat
who patrolled the thirty-two corners of the house.

She occupied the place in my absence and my presence,
eating and licking her paws, shedding her undercoat

as winter folded back into spring, and insects and stray bats returned
as fodder for her games of cruelty. She knew nothing

of my nephew and the noose he slipped around his neck,
leaning forward while seated on the floor,

until the life was strangled from him
and he was found among his store of guns, a long knife,

the tight black clothing that he wore. Outside, Portland
kept winding past, with its bicycles and beer, pretty bridges

spanning a river whose name I don't even know, a city image
of perpetual immaturity fixed like a young man

strained against a rope. Hope didn't live there,
with him, in the clapboard house he shared,

and for some time it didn't live with me either.
The cat didn't mind, winding behind the woodstove

in the fall, when the first cold night sent me to split
some kindling and warm the old stones of the hearth.

She didn't care about anything other than herself
and in this there was perfection—to eat and sleep,

to find amusement in the hunt, to seek out the slant
of sunlight where it warmed the clean pine floors,

and to meet me when I came home,
in a way that resembled love, how she came running—

hearing my key turn the tumblers of the lock,
even though I had trained her to link

the sound of my arrival with the food
I would spill into her bowl.

There was bliss in this, to be met by a body
at the door, to be joined at night

in a bed, her head within my reach,
inside which no words tumbled, no reasoning

wrecked the morning, no memory
bound the missing to my single body

left lying nightly in the bed.
In the morning I rise up again to go out

into the world, forgetting whatever images
flickered through the dim chambers

of house or brain, bed and book and hearth,
the smoke rising up from the stove embers

which, in the morning chill
and with my black tools,

I stir back into warming life.

ELEGY FOR A HANGED BOY

Your white body drifts outside the frame
somewhere beyond the reaches of concern.

You died in Portland with a noose around your neck, alone.
When you were an infant I held you on my chest,

gripped your arm when you were a little older.
Later still, I watched you eat the dinner I cooked from food

that grew and ripened one summer in the yard—
your smoke particles now sunstruck and pacific.

This morning I turn you out, push against
the clouded thought you have become,

but you come back when I turn my face into the pillow,
exiled though you are to the wind's country

stirring the upper orders of the air.
I know now that ghosts, indeed, exist

but they are not what you expect.
They are nothing but a mood you cannot shake—

the dust that dulls the edges of the mirror
to darken the bruise of the day.

III.

THE INDIFFERENCE OF HORSES

after Giorgio di Chirico's Due cavalli in riva al mare

As a boy I had two horses—a mare and a gelding.

The mare was old, with a white coat and mane—gray,

in the language of horsemen. The gelding I bought as a yearling

and was a roan and white pinto. Both were Arabians

and had the large, expressive eyes of the breed.

They were stabled at home, and I cared for them

with a devotion like that of a father to his children.

The mare was the more elegant of the two

and more patient, though she grew sour in the presence

of other horses, and accepted the gelding with grudging

tolerance and outbursts of temper. The gelding

was tall and flashy, with pert ears

and the slight Roman nose of a Saddlebred,

and when I handled him, he had the habit

of pushing me with his head, or nuzzling my pockets

looking for food. I spent hours in their quiet company

brushing their coats, picking muck from their hooves

and when a farrier hit my mare across the back with a rasp

for fidgeting, I shouted at him, paid him, and told him to leave.

When I mounted my horses

I underwent a transformation. From atop their backs

I surveyed the world, which now seemed traversable,

rather than bound by the bluffs crowding our valley farm.

Astride them, I became a new creature—

powerful, elegant, capable of speed—and the exhibitions

I entered offered opportunities for costuming.

That they were, at times, unpredictable, made the experience

of riding a dynamic one, in which the mind and the horse's body

were at odds, which of course was much like the relationship

of my mind with my own body. Mostly I was silent when I rode,

though sometimes I spoke to the animals in clicks,

murmurs, low warning vowels, and this sublingual exchange

was an intimacy verging on the sexual.

Together or apart, my horses conveyed a solitude I came to admire.

I wondered at its source—was it their size and strength

that made them so content in themselves? Their animal brains

that were free of anxiety? Was it beauty that made them

turn inward and into themselves? I came to love them

for what I did not know about them—their secret moods,

what they knew or didn't know. There was also

the vexing condition of their indifference to me

as it taught me a sharp lesson

about the harder arrangements of affection,

it being possible to love another being with one's fullest self,

and see how that love could be absorbed,

lived with, accepted even—and not have that feeling returned.

PORTRAIT OF MARY MAGDALENE

after Piero della Francesca

On the road to Arezzo, the prostitutes

have set up their stations—a white plastic lawn chair

and a dusty spot with enough room for a driver

to pull over and inquire about the price. I suppose

they take their customers back into the woods

where an old mattress lies under a little roof of tin

and where the passing cars muffle the animal yelp

of a man's cum-cry. Meanwhile, in a church in town,

the rendition of the Magdalene stares down at us

from the Renaissance, but doesn't see, being nothing

but paint mixed into plaster. The artist has rendered her

with the soft lips and eyes of a farm girl, tented

her wide hips in pleats of green. He gave her

a cloak of red and white—partly thrown back,

partly pulled up to cover her newfound modesty,

her hair still wet from drying the feet

of a man who didn't want to hold her down

until he'd had enough, her face still dusty

from her station at the side of the road.

This is a portrait of kindness and contrition,

shame already fading as her hair begins to dry,

and this man takes her with him like a bride.

He is nowhere to be seen in the fresco—just her—

her seven demons already ground out into the dirt,

tossed like pots of night soil in the ditch.

On the road the women are still at work, cheap jewelry

catching a glint of the sun, high shoes improbable

for a walk into the woods, as one woman

casts down her cigarette and grinds

its ember in the dirt. And where am I in all this?

A spectator thrilled or shocked a little,

my own demons still coursing through

the red riot of my veins, hidden

in the wet cave of my mouth like a man

I've caught in the back of my throat

until I spit his essence in the dust.

It is said Mary Magdalene boarded

a miraculous ship and rode it all the way to France.

There she died as a hermit in a cave

her hair grown long and gray. Her skull

can be seen there in a church. It's a holy thing,

though the reliquary preserves the decay

on which the contours of flesh

once formed a beloved face.

FRAGMENT OF ST. JULIAN

after Piero della Francesca

The throat of the stag was never meant for speaking.

It would have pained the creature to make the shapes,

to force the tongue and push against its single row of teeth,

make way for the warning to Julian, whose arrow

broke the bleeding hole the spirit of speech went in.

The first the beast spoke was warning, threat, and pain,

which is the way of all first language, the mouth

opening in surprise, the lungs seizing up to bark.

In the fragment of wall skimmed off and framed,

Julian too looks pained, regret not yet registered,

understanding leaking like a tint stirred into plaster

his cloak still pulled around his shoulders, his club

gripped in his good hand, having beaten to death

the bodies of those who made him. Regret would come later,

but for now he was more animal than that talking beast

who knew him for what he was.

ICE MAN

Born from the ice, he was born again
and into a world, rough and cold,

as unkind and kind as the one
he left behind on a day in fall,

when he fell from the arrow
lodged in his back, and someone

came upon him to bash in his skull
and finish the job for good. His murderer

left him lying there, and did not
rob the corpse, let him keep

possession of his valuable copper axe
in reach of his newly useless hand, left his tools

strapped to his body now cooling on the top of an alp.
His last meal of grain and roast goat

stilled in his gut. No animals came
to feed on his flesh, no people came

to bury him. That night the sun set
then rose, and set again ten thousand times,

and the man froze and thawed,
and the glacier wrapped him in a counterpane of ice.

His hand reached toward the glittering sky,
the mountain's chilled tongue pressed into his hardening mouth,

and so he went on into the centuries
that went on without him, but which would not let him go.

Below him and leagues away
Rome rose and burned and rose again;

the Trojans practiced their maneuvers in the sun,
and they too died away just as the Sybil

said they would. The alp kept him
beyond speech, and beyond pain,

beyond avarice and regret. Kept
his last day legible to anyone who looked,

for its testament of violence shot into his back.
Now he lies in state,

hovering on a bed of glass, and can be looked at
like the body of a saint.

Through the vitrine window
he is more a joint of smoked meat,

a skin bag dragged into place by the ice.
His lip curls up to show the ivory teeth

that bit down on a thousand clouds.
Around him, the Bozeners keep pouring their beer,

selling their fruit in sacks on the square,
while their dogs sleep under restaurant tables

before they tighten the slack leashes
binding them to men, and lead

their keepers away.

MUSEUM OF BEES

At the museum of bees, there are no bees—
just the empty boxes of the hives

painted gaily, offered as folk art
and displayed here in this ancient farmhouse—

picturesque on the slope of an alpine meadow,
with its thatched roof, and its valuable view,

its fallow fields mowed periodically
to keep the best alpine flowers in bloom.

The bee boxes smell of warm wax, a whiff
of honey with its faint trace of chamomile,

and in the part of the museum that shows
how the farmers once lived, there is a glass case

containing a doll with a porcelain head,
its marble eyes black and unblinking, staring upward

at a heaven fixed in its unseeing gaze.
I assume this is the Christ child

reproduced for domestic veneration,
and I admire its human hair

which is tow-colored and curled in spiral
locks that fall around its matte china-gray face.

Someone sewed a swaddling gown
from strips of silk and lace. On a bed

of brocade, the little body lies
sealed in its coffin of glass. Outside

on the sun-cast meadow, hikers
traverse the trail on their way past

this forgotten house, hidden in a cluster of trees,
the bees too having been forgotten

or left to make their own way
wild in the domesticated woods, and far

from the diligent hands of men.

FREELOVE, DISCARNATE

Under a mantle of snow,

under moss, sand and gravel,

under roots and schist, five feet of thin soil,

under the sanded pine boards of an undersized coffin,

under lace, under linen, shift poked with eyelets,

under a curtain of hair tied up for the afterlife,

cap stitched by sore fingers of a sister,

under powdery skin, bone softened by acid,

blood gone black as the water dried away,

lies the desiccated heart of Freelove Hancox

who perished some time two centuries ago.

Her remaining purchase on the world of the living

is this headstone, dateless, spackled with lichen,

wheeled over by gulls, those persistent omnivores,

prayed over by wind blown in off the bay.

What lies beneath this minimal marker?

What lingers in the folds of her funerary dress?

No secret note folded in a reticule,

mourning ring lost under an auction-house floor?

The truth of her is chiseled into stone—

not my fantasy of her costume, but a name

once spoken over her infant head

presiding now over six feet of ground, which I find one morning

pushing past the gate wrought by a blacksmith,

set with care into a wall of granite

here in a cemetery in Stonington, Connecticut.

PROPOSITION

That the smell of cows drifting in the open window is, indeed, that of a living beast.

That I too am a living beast.

That the body I possess is inhabited only by me.

That my body is neither at rest nor occupied by dramatic motion.

That I am, by my best account, fully alive.

That the room in which I am seated is in Germany, in a town called Worpswede.

That a poet I admire once lived here too, though he is long since dead.

Rilke wrote, "That I gently wipe away the look of suffered injustice sometimes
     hinders the pure motion of spirits a little."

That there are such things as "spirits."

That we were born suffering, but that we are not meant to suffer.

That the wind blows and the birches outside my window sing a little.

And that cooing and chucking of the dove I hear is also a kind of song.

That the difference between the living and the dead is mostly one of conjugation.

Er starb. Er ist gestorben. Ein gestorbenes Mensch.

That what we make when we speak is a kind of music, but disjointed
     and that music seeks a unity that our speech does not possess.

Once I felt as though I was dead, but now the reasons for that feeling baffle me.

I marvel at what it is to feel the sun on my skin.

"Burnish," is the word that comes into my head.

"Burnished by the sun," as if my torso was a copper shield.

That my torso is a kind of shield protecting the inside from the outside.

Though we all know we are penetrable in many ways.

UNPAINTED PICTURES
after Emil Nolde

WINDMILL, FRIESLAND

An X of a windmill pins the sky to the land.
A road sets off, generally seaward.
Why does the horizon tell its story
of nearness and distance
by dividing the world with its single black line?
And the clouds? What of those?
They are water. Just like this paint.
Only today, both are tinted red—blood red—
like an animal stain—
drying under a weakening sun.

LANDSCAPE WITH LAKE

The Lake reflects the sky's spreading face.
At the little farmhouse, someone has forgotten
to close the pasture gate. But no matter—
the cows were sold last autumn when the hay was bad.
The sun declines, letting the lake's face redden
with no one but you and me to care.

BLUE GREEN SEA WITH SMALL STEAMSHIP

Black boat with its rusty smoke
knows the sea and the sky aren't the same.
The old man stoked the furnace
until he couldn't lift a shovel.
I'm the only one who remembers him much
with Uncle in his grave
and Mother determined not to.
He was often cruel, but he made me laugh,
usually at my own expense.
All those boats are long since sold for scrap.
Some days arrive with what feels like hope
and the sky bleeds gold like a flame.

THE BEAST OF BRAY ROAD

Whelped in a den of timothy and fur
pulled from the belly of my dam,

I nursed and grew on the blue milk
drawn by my suckling urge. Born white,

I darkened as I aged, the softer fell on my back
coarsening as I learned to hunt.

With my sibling, I began to track the deer,
find where the fawns were sleeping

under their temporary spotted hides, as if
that could conceal them from our superiority,

their mothers wide-eyed and helpless
to our assaults, snorting with sorrow

as we cracked the fawn's soft bones larded
with greasy marrow. Years went by

hunting and sleeping, rolling together
in the dust of our cunning den.

In winter, we mostly slept—us three
back to belly to back,

our hole in the sandstone bank occluded
with brush, the snow muffling and tamping down

the earth one icy star at a time.
One spring we awoke in hunger

and I watched as my brother
hardened into himself, went off alone,

became sullen, slinking off to the pond,
and licking his part that was angry and red

when he thought nobody saw.
Mornings went by when he did not return

leaving me alone to sleep the day away.
My loneliness rose like a planet.

I began to follow him, practicing
the softest motion of my paws,

willing the birds into silence.
I watched as he stepped gingerly

onto the plowed springtime field
which we were instructed to avoid.

I followed, but he kept driving me back,
turning to snap when I got too close,

then loping ahead, singing under his breath.
When had he learned what music was?

From our leafy kingdom in the trees, I watched
as he galloped across the field where we

had seen men and their reek-cloud
of artificiality. There at what was called

a road, he stopped, looking up to the sky's hot eye,
then rose up on his hind two legs

and walked in the world of men.
I remained behind. Many seasons came and went,

our mother crumbled into an afterthought of dust,
my hidden world more hidden

as men forget how to hunt.
I have seen the forest thicken, the sky warm

and change, birds arrive whose calls are foreign to my ear.
I do not know where my brother has gone

but I do know that he left me here
to prey upon myself alone.

THE BATS

I share my house with a colony of bats.
They live in the roof peak,
enter through a gap.

At dusk they fly out, dip
into inverted arcs
to catch what flutters or stings,

what can only be hunted at night.
Sunlight stops their flight,
drives them into their hot chamber

to rest and nest, troll-faces
pinched shut. I hear them scratch.
In darkness they chop and hazard through the sky,

around blue outlines of pines,
pitch up over the old Dutch house
we share. They scare some

but not me. I see them
for what they seem—
timid, wee, happy or lucky,

pinned to the roof beams,
stitched up in their ammonia reek
and private as dreams.

FIVE COLD STORIES

Reykjavik, Iceland

> "Now you must have no more kisses," she said, "or I should
> kiss you to death."
>> *from* The Snow Queen *by Hans Christian Andersen*

In Iceland, I put my hand inside a man. It was a sexual act. He lived in a black
tower overlooking the sea. Snow crowned the mountains, and out his window the
aurora pulled its ragged curtain of light across the night sky. It is interesting to
feel the bones move inside a man. Interesting too his pulse. I cannot say I was
sexually stimulated, rather the atmosphere was stimulating. You must understand,
I was being generous; I followed his instructions carefully and with something
resembling love. I wore a latex glove and nothing else. His bedroom was spare and
elegant in the Nordic fashion, and he kept the chains of his sling tightened with
tape, so the ringing of the links would remain unobtrusive. In drawers with pads to
prevent slippage his tools were arranged as precious objects. Sweet were his lips and
sweet the taste of night, skin white and warm, flushed pink at the neck. How had
I come to this bony island heated by molten rock, hand in a man above my wrist? I
imagined myself reading, alone or with a cat balled on my lap, little body and brain
familiar to the fingers. Later, we stood on the street as morning broke against the
shore, having reassembled our faces. He touched my coat. When Petur spoke, he
stammered and I leaned closer so as to better attend his mouth.

Haukijärvi, Sweden

> "You are so clever," said the reindeer. "I know you can tie all
> the winds of the world with a piece of twine."
> *from* The Snow Queen *by Hans Christian Andersen*

Nasti, Gargolas, Liidneoaivii, Skaolbmenjunni tied to birch saplings, digging in the snow. With hooves wide as salad plates, they paw to form a basin into which they fold themselves and lie down in their bowl of ice. They are not kind. They are not our friends. They are not unkind. They would not exist without us. By day Skaolbmenjunni pulls my sled. I harness him in the morning and he shakes his antlers to chase me off, but I persist and buckle the colorful girth around his ribs. His hair is hollow and cold to the touch and smells of animal secrets. In my pocket I carry the meal of the day which is smoked reindeer wrapped in bread. I pull my sled and place it behind him, his head bound, pull the birch rods to either side and clip them in the hooks, my hands freezing to the metal before I can shove them into the fur mittens. Jonas will lead us with Nasti, and let his reindeer loose, holding the long rein and jumping onto his sled with a small hop. My deer will tear after him, anxious and strong, bounding through snow to follow. On the trail there is no speaking, only the clacking of the sled poles and the clicking of the hooves as the rear hits the dewclaw of the front, the runners creaking in their tracks, and the bellows of reindeer lungs pumping into the air with a woof.

At night we sleep on boughs of spruce, our breath crusting the canvas of the tent. I bury my hands in the fur of the hide where I will lie, my breath steaming, the wolverine lake indifferent to the wan somnambulant sun. Outside the reindeer grunt and sigh, listen to our quiet talking rising up the flue with the smoke. We boil coffee and make confessions under the Aurora, the sky aswirl with the icy chips of stars. Star Face, Escape Artist, White Head, Roman Nose tied to birch saplings, digging in the snow.

Hämeenkyrö, Finland

> the boat's on a pike's shoulders
> on a water-dog's haunches!
> > *from* The Kalevala *by Elias Lönnrot*

Miners, understanding the cold, reached the bottom of the lake by removing one centimeter of ice a day. Each night the lake would freeze below it and another inch was chipped away. After a time, the ice stairs could be used and precious metals drawn from the sandy floor. At night, the lake would glow from lanterns burning under ice.

In Helsinki, a man fed me a piece of pike from the silver tines of a fork. He held it forward and I had to reach out my tongue to keep it from falling. The morsel was fine and nourished the senses. We spoke the common tongue, which was my own, and that night he clucked his tongue in a sound of pleasure as I pushed inside him—no language, muscle sucked with its secrets and accents, which is the sound of the land held in the mouth.

People stream to the tram, babies in down sacks in their prams and white fur, pushed through the cold like Romanovs. They smile at their keepers with faces from icons.

James, I lit a candle for your ailing spine, one for your lungs, one for your serrated tongue. The patriarchs stared as I touched the wick to the oil aflame in its central ring. I bought the beeswax candles from a young man wearing an old man's suit, which was tan and showed its age at the elbows. He made change on a little tray so as not to touch my hand.

Each day, the sun grows a little stronger, but I relish the bitter bite in my nostrils, my eyelashes crisped white beneath a ruff of fox.

Hämeenkyrö, Finland

It flew like a little bird
its bright border gleaming
from "Mourning Cloak" by Göran Sonnevi

In Jonas's story, the old woman comes out the door of the abandoned house to throw her pail of water onto the snow. No one lived in the village, and so the sight startled him. He told his father, and his father told him no one has lived in the village for twenty years.

A year later he met a woman—a tourist—who had found her way to the same village, and had seen the same woman throw her water on the snow. She told this story unbidden, to Jonas's surprise.

Jonas pronounces the letter "j" as though it were a "y." Lingonberry Yam. Long Yahns. At night Jonas and I share a cabin where we lie facing each other in opposite bunks. I try not to stare as he undresses, opting instead for discreet glances as he strips off his final layer of wool and sits cross-legged in his shorts as the stove beats heat into the room, and his hairless skin warms pink in the flush of heat. "If you need, it is only to ask." "According to me, he is a struggly boy." "This latch it is a little bit special." "It is an awkward smell." He describes the chopping blade, the ear-marking blade, and the blade for everything else. "It is three kilometers the bird way."

During the day, Jonas sits atop his sled and uses a pole to guide his deer, leaning from side to side, waving his arms to direct the beast forward. Snow sags from the spruce, pulls the heads of birches to the ground in arcs throughout the forest. We watch for dogs which the deer despise, and we watch for other reindeer which move through the forests digging for moss, and appearing and disappearing at will. No other creatures are out in the frightful March cold, though the sun has begun its return.

An old woman busies herself in the winter quarters. Why are the dogs so quiet? She must make up the fire, the grate is growing cold. Who is that who wanders in the road? Why the clatter, why the cold chime? With her burden, she steps into welcoming air.

Hämeenkyrö, Finland

> At last they came to the Finmark, and knocked at the Finn
> woman's chimney, for she hadn't a sign of a door.
> *from* The Snow Queen *by Hans Christian Andersen*

At the sauna, the women lean their heads together and murmur. They wear sturdy swimwear and plastic clogs and knit caps. On the benches we sweat in the low light, while a man dips water from the reservoir with a neat scoop on a pole, filling the air with steam. The heat is personal and draws you into yourself, hands over your face to keep from burning. On the benches we lean forward, the air filling with our inner water.

In Finnish a woman directs us to follow her; she is bossy and has the authority of a captain. Through the chambers we exit into the night, the paths ice-covered and slick. We follow her sturdy body to the pier where we turn to face the others and, gripping the rails, lower ourselves through the hole in the ice into the black water. We leave our heat behind, sent to the bottom of the lake, the body filled and emptied, burnished pink and infantile.

An old man tells me he loves books and he reads a great deal while he takes off his clothes. He wears a string of wooden beads around his neck and puts a small wool cap upon his head. He is lean and robust, hairless, skin and flesh firm. I admire him. He carries a green bottle, corked and half full of a mysterious silted drink.

We duck into the smoke sauna, a blackened cabin over baking stones. We darken and stoop under a roof of soot. The stove is our mother pushing her heat onto us, pouring it onto us, dizzying and irradiating the pink spiders of our lungs, searing the bottoms of our feet, heat and ice, heat and ice, the lake keeps the eye of night at the bottom, the mouth of winter is the hole we climb into, jagged with teeth of ice. The mind blinds itself, scorched and frozen, dumb to thought. The body seeks the extreme. Cool me and heat me, cool and heat, Mother remake me, here in the snow.

IV.

ON THE AUTOBIOGRAPHICAL IMPULSE

An Account

Does it matter that I am homosexual, and therefore on the edge

of some larger portion of the human world?

Does it matter that my name is German, and that Germans find my name amusing?

Does it matter that my mother's family was poor?

That her father beat my grandmother when he drank? Does it matter that he
    fled Kansas

during the Dust Bowl to ride the rails? Does it matter that his aunts and uncles

were herded into Siberia by the hand of Stalin, shot on the banks of the Black Sea?

Does it matter that they believed in ghosts, ate lard and sugar sandwiches,

went into the service, went to sea? Does it matter that I have family in Chile,

in Argentina, Transylvania, Hungary? Does it matter that my parents

turned against me when I was nineteen? That I worked as a prostitute in Greece,

groomed horses for a baron and let myself be fucked by weekend guests

in payment for my stay at the beach? Does it matter that I worked in a factory?

Does it matter that I know how to hunt, field dress a deer, knit a sweater,

make a basket, pollard willows, converse in three languages, read four?

Does it matter that my nephew believed he was being watched

by the police, that aliens bedeviled his nights, that he loved mycology and weapons of all sorts, that he tattooed the outline

of Minnesota on his chest, and that the noose he used to hang himself

was put out that week in the trash?

Does it matter that he lived, or that he died?

How much of what we are is what is seen? Am I more tender

because I am penetrable? How many men have been inside my body?

I lost count. Their ghosts would know. Does it matter that I light candles

in churches to burn away disbelief? Does it matter that I sit

behind a desk in a room lined with books, that people come

to hear me speak? Does it matter that my body repels me

but that I like my hair? Does vanity matter?

Outside, the wind turns and the sun burns the grass

as it has always done. I understand

the moon to be a cliché, yet it still lodges into the sky at night,

and the moths search out the truth of the bedside lamp.

Some will survive the night;

others I will sweep from the bedside table

where they spent their last hours yearning toward the light.

On Victimhood

Once, I was made the victim of a man.

He beat me the way a boxer might beat a bag of sawdust.

That afternoon, my world became very small, centered

on the bruised surface of my face. I thought that day,

as I shrank from his attentions,

that I would die there, strangled on my bed, while outside

in the California fog, the lone palm below my window

rattled in the Pacific wind, indifferent to my plight.

This too I survived, as the man

grew bored or scared, and simply put on his clothes and left.

Having been a victim, I am not a victim.

Despite what you think you know,

you know nothing of the words I have used

to empty myself of myself. This event means less to me

with each morning, and even when it occurred, it meant very little,

the man not knowing who I was.

Today I am seated at an ugly desk in a beautiful room.

Large shutters open onto a medieval courtyard.

The occasions of my life conspired to bring me here

on a September morning in Umbria. Jackdaws rustle

in the olive trees. Workmen grind stone with a machine.

Behind us is a summer of violence, which moved around the globe

popping up in corners, unexpected, always, but anticipated

nonetheless. A man drove a truck through a crowd.

A man was shot while facedown on the ground,

and a tyrant rose in the West.

Violence is the hand shifting the gears of a truck,

a mind fixed on the density of a crowd.

The fog burns off and is already forgotten

except by the lines on this page.

On Living with Animals

I spent a week riding horses in the mountains.

Each day it was my job to saddle a new beast,

slip a bit into its reluctant mouth, then tighten the strap at its chin.

After brushing off the mud, I put the saddle on

and cinched the girth. Sometimes the horse would suck in its breath,

to keep me from pulling too tight. I would slip my left foot into the stirrup, and step up to straddle the broad, accepting back. From atop the horse

I could see across the vast lands sometimes mounded in hillocks of grass,

sometimes black with sand. The horse and I agreed on the proceedings

and we set out in search of the wind. It met us, each and every day,

a thing we experienced together, brushing over our faces and pulling back our hair.

The horse's heat drew up into my legs

and my hands tangled in its mane. Sometimes we galloped, or crossed streams,

once we swam a deep river, my boots filling, the horse keeping me

steady on its back. It could have thrown me easily, but it didn't.

It kept me there, my presence whether a burden or a comfort

it's impossible to say.

Sky Burial

Darkness drew on, though the sun was shining.

The darkness was on the inside, an oily film

smoking the glass of what I would call my "soul."

From my station inside the house I watched

as vultures took away in mouthfuls the body of an animal

I had shot days before. They hopped about the yard,

clipped themselves onto the branches of the wild cherry.

I sometimes heard them roosting on the copper roof ridge,

their talons scabbering along. Vultures are patient birds,

but adamant. First one came, then a dozen, perhaps more.

Their presence was disturbing, as was their smell,

but they gave to me the idea of a sky burial.

So I practiced for two days in the yard,

holding the loaded gun to my chest or to my temple,

fitting the open barrel into my mouth,

clicking it past my teeth. The metal was cold

and tasted of acrid oil, but I welcomed it,

as though I were tasting the ardent tongue of a lover.

There are those who think that objects have a will—

that their realization of form creates a kind of yearning

to fulfill the purpose of that form. In those days

I can tell you that I felt the gun drawing toward me—

a kind of subtle leaning—

the hard walnut stock asking to be stroked and taken up,

the barrel in my mouth sexual and full of need—so obvious

it resists this explanation. *Use me*, the gun said.

You are not as important as you think. Use me

and I will send my carrion-stinking vultures

to pull you apart and carry you into the sky.

On the third day, when I picked up the gun

I saw the face of my mother.

She came to mind and stayed there,

taking up space in the bleak room inside me.

Once present, she would not leave. Her love

for me has, for the fifty years of my life,

even empty as I was and as ugly as I had become,

remained steadfast. She is the force that stopped me

from ending my own life.

What have I achieved? Is this the music you hoped for?

Perhaps you have long since put this text away—I'll never know.

As it turns out, my instinct for survival has been strong.

I have stood at the threshold of a vast emptiness, or been held to it

and forced to look down. From that ledge,

I was called back to the living more than once.

My presence here is testament

to the mind's ability to correct itself.

I am living, even if some days, it is more than I can bear.

I am here, the sun crossing in shadows over the hills.

MIDSUMMER

I am standing up on the hill crest—no—
I am recalling being on the hill crest yesterday

as the bee-eater broke from the trees,
fanned out and tipped a branch to stalk a fat bee

dipping onto the long grass of a pasture where
I had stopped and crouched down, having run

up the hill, pressed two fingers to the throb
in my throat to feel the treasure of my blood

flood through fresh with oxygen, fresh with air
I pulled in, pushed out, permeable as the hive

I watch at the edge of the grove, the bees flung out
into the sun. My only life is being spent—today—

the longest day of the year, here on a hill looking out
for a moment and feeling my body unearthed,

feeling it fall, foot by foot, all the weight of me
moving side to side as I run now on the flat past a farm

where three dogs break from the hedge
to bark. The youngest one makes a show of it,

then follows, running ahead of me, running behind
and to the left, into the woods at the side of the road

emerging further on, turning his head to see
that I am still there, and so we play a bit,

this dog and I, its foxy face and dirty coat
running the road, conversing with my pace and step,

this steep incline now up to the broken tower
tipped at the top of the hill. This today is the middle

day of the middle portion of what may be my
middle years. The tower marks the center,

tilting slightly one way or another, indicating an end,
which, of course, it must. This is what happens

to a man of fifty who has no wife, no child whose face
reflects his past, the cheekbones bred somewhere

on the Russian steppe, the hair his mother washed
and cut, skin that browns in the sun,

bones that knit and eyes the blank blue of some forgotten well.
My future is the only future, my past a story or a scar,

a body, a book, a bed to rest my head in. Alone today
I am alone. Alone in my thoughts I am alive on this hill,

the tower a structure leaning in ruin, the dog another body
breathing the air, smelling yesterday's rain, the bees

working through the day to bring in the beauty of sun
and flower, pollen and the sweet essence of olive.

On the trail, over a wire fence, comes the sound of bells
tinny and small, familiar, a herd of goats browsing

in the green, their black horns dipping down,
bells making a circle of sound as they raise up their heads

all at once to see what I am—a man at the fence,
their ears flicked toward me, gazes fixed, until they discern

I intend them no harm, and they continue
on their way through the grass.

TO WHOM IT MAY CONCERN:

In the Polaroid in a drawer of the house
the other relatives picked over, I'm the blur in the background,

mop of silvery hair. The rasp of the ashpan when you empty the stove
is a bit like my voice, stuck in the chimney like a nest.

You won't have to know how I procrastinated, of my abiding fear
of snakes, or how I gave terrible presents when I bothered to give them at all.

I was told by a psychic to remember the unloved dead,
and so I did, but not in a way they would like,

recalling how they got ugly when they drank
or stole the loose change from the laundry

when they thought nobody saw. I spent years
writing my last letters, writing off the debt of a cold bed,

pretending I was busy when really I was home
pinned to the couch by a cat.

For money I did many things—trapped muskrats,
forged thank-you notes, let men pet me while I danced.

Mostly I played the role of someone who cared,
tilted in my chair and trying to appear engaged,

the preoccupied uncle you weren't quite sure you liked.
That's me smoking in the Winnebago, leaving the sink

clean of hair. I'm there deadheading the rhubarb
nobody bothers to pick and my worthless collections—

rag rugs, concrete gnomes—
were most likely put out in the trash.

Sometimes I lied when I was bored. I wanted you
to know what I knew, though I eventually gave that up

preferring to make you laugh.
This life I led was mostly private, and hours were spent

sweeping bat guano from a crumbling set of stairs.
Nobody knew the half of it, and nobody seemed to care.

I foresaw how neglected the town cemetery became,
glimpsed in a vision the rusted fence that let in the deer.

They stripped the bark from the junipers
that eventually came down in a storm.

I was in that storm, blown out across the ice
toward Arcadia. That's a town in Wisconsin

and not some name for paradise.